PANDEMIC POEMS,
MAYORALTY
——— *The Perfect Recipe* ———

PANDEMIC POEMS, MAYORALTY

The Perfect Recipe

Written by Len Thomas

BOLTON MAYOR'S CONSORT

It is 2020 and we are living in exceptional times facing difficult challenges such as staying in good health. COVID-19 makes us cautious and has transformed normality. We question and wonder what will the new normal be. We are all doing our best to support Voluntary Services, Charities, Care Workers, the NHS and other Key Workers. The COVID-19 Pandemic has highlighted how dependent we are on others to provide the necessities of life.

The new Mayoralty emerges into this frightening scenario and appreciates the excellent work voluntary groups do in wide and varied circumstances. Much of this work comes under the auspices of key members of The Bolton Family, so dedicated and unstinting in what they achieve.

As Mayor together with my Consort, husband Len, we hope to raise vast sums of money in our 'Year of The Volunteer'. To further this cause, I challenged my Consort to write at least a poem a week during our Mayoralty. All the proceeds raised from this book will enhance resources for our charities. We have had to think of these innovative ways to support the charitable groups.

Please get behind the quest and support our charities.

URBAN OUTREACH
BACKUP
HALLIWELL BEFRIENDING SERVICE
FORTALICE
THE OCTAGON

My sincerest thanks and best wishes to you all,

Linda Thomas

THE MAYOR OF BOLTON

'Come into our Parlour!'

It would be usual practice to welcome people into the Mayor's Parlour to enjoy the beautiful, regal room at Bolton Town Hall. However the pandemic has meant sadly we have had to close it's doors to the public. For now here is a sneak preview. We hope to be able to welcome you here again in 2021.

Introducing Pandemic Poems

The COVID-19 pandemic has changed Bolton life, in fact the world, dramatically. Under these socially protected months, I, the Mayor's Consort, was shielded. I have always had a love for poetry and to give me a focus during this tough period, the Mayor set me the challenge of writing a poem a day in Lockdown. This has resulted in a poetic compilation with all proceeds going to the Mayor's charities.

Poetry and Verse are personal and contain my emotional views about various situations and events. You may wish to share my interpretation and hopefully this will not detract from your understanding of these experiences.

These poems reflect my inner depths and are expressions of the moods surrounding personal events. On looking back, putting these literary creations into perspective, I realise my judgements were influenced by how I felt at that specific time. I hope my words evoke feelings that you can relate to either as a parent, grandparent, son, daughter or relative and become personal to you.

If you are fortunate or unfortunate to be married, or connected to someone in public life, then I sympathise; but also point out to you that your relationship is enriched, your experiences enhanced, and your patience tested. Remember, at the end of the day, you are to be supportive, understanding and someone who will break the monotony of sometimes, thankless public life. In this scenario, as the Mayor's Consort I accepted her challenge and produced 75 poems now, before you.

Len Thomas

BOLTON MAYOR'S CONSORT

Contents

We Have Only Just Begun

May 15, 2020 the Mayoralty's just begun
Mayor and Consort welcome everyone
To celebrate the 'Year of Volunteers and Carers'.
Join us one and all and be their standard bearers
We have composed many an ode
Hopefully to be read in many an abode.
Businesses and Employers join the craze
Of fundraising madness in the Bolton maze.
Let's hope we augment our charitable load
To spend Bolton wide and just down the road.
So, rise fellow Boltonians, promote the Volunteer
Who we all hold in our hearts so dear.

Bolton's First Citizen

Her Public Service began back in 1988,
Representing Westhoughton seemed like fate.
She served with pleasure young and old,
Families trusted her so bold.
She did much for Howfen's Early Years,
Dedicated nurture and the pleasure hers.
Many a delightful story she can tell
About days serving Howfen and Halliwell.
For over thirty years or more now
She's been a representative with knowhow,
Solving numerous confidential cases
Meeting people from many places.
As First Citizen it is a pleasure to serve you all
And despite Covid-19, we must stand tall.
We have suffered tragedy and pain
But there will be better times again.

Former Mayoralty Pair Bows Out

The former Mayor and Consort have gone.
So, thanks Hillary Bows and Banjo Don.
You have been a very special unique pair,
Welcoming and being welcomed everywhere.
Always cordial, wearing a smiling face,
Lighting up the room in every place.
Raising thousands for Charity most of all,
Who can forget that fantastic Mayor's Ball?
You have been hardworking and revered all year
So for now, it is au revoir and not adieu.
A million thankyous and so on
For you Hillary Bows and Banjo Don!

My Wife: From Councillor to Mayor

The Councillor, my wife leads a hectic life
With lots of hassle and strife.
It's heaven alone without her phone
And that monotonous ringtone.
It brings a smile for a while
Away from hassle and strife,
That's my wife and public life.
She has plenty of nerve to serve
To help others with a smile
Exuding elegance and guile.
She hides the hassle and strife
Being now the Mayor, my wife
What a life!

Honour to Serve You All

Public servant to the end,
Many meetings to attend,
No complaints, a duty to uphold,
Practical, persuasive, calm and cool,
Believed to be respected as a rule.
To serve others has been her goal,
With honesty and purity of soul.
To give and seldom to receive,
To be truthful and never to deceive.
The ultimate professional, dedicated, warm,
Always approachable, ready to inform.
She exhibits justice and goodwill.
Tactful, respectful, calm and tranquil,
Composed, relaxed and caring too
We appreciate representatives like you.

The Mayor's Charities

Fortalice, Urban Outreach and Backup,
Octagon Theatre and Befriending Service Halliwell
Local charities whose funds we'd like to swell,
So read about them all and tell
The gradely folk of Bolton to give a dime
Enabling the town's less fortunate a better time
To enjoy the essentials of life,
Alleviating much turmoil and strife

Virtual Mayoralty for Now

Is there anyone there?
And do you care?
If you do,
We need you!
Don't be shy,
Don't walk by,
Show your face,
In a Virtual Place,
So that we can see
That you want to be
Raising lots of money
And milk and honey
For the Mayor's Charity Pot
Come grab your slot.

Backup

You bring hope, aspiration to young people and the homeless,
With all the resilience and confidence, GOD can bless,
Providing youngsters with shelter and a house,
Giving them coaching, mentoring and the nous
To feel uplifted and inspired to live
A controlled life willing to accept and give
Support to those less fortunate than you,
Creating self-belief and self-esteem long overdue.
You're given a home not just a roof over your head,
A safe haven and a warm, comfortable bed.
Born from Bolton's Young Persons' Scheme
Backup makes life real not just living a dream.

The Young Octagon

Dance, dance, whoever you are
Nearby in Bolton or from afar.
Community youngsters on the stage,
All types of abilities of any age.
The Octagon Theatre giving them a start
Growing in confidence as they develop their art.

Halliwell Befriending Service

Visiting me today...Hip hip hooray!
Peeping through the curtain,
Seeing you arrive for certain,
Keeping me company and in touch,
Love you ever so much.
No longer on my own nor apart,
Love you all from my heart.
Thank you for being there
And showing that you really care
Visiting me today...Hip hip hooray!

Fortalice

For women, families experiencing violence,
Fortalice is Bolton's haven, free from malice.
Safe for those affected's use,
Sheltered from domestic abuse.
Peace and tranquility after the alarm
Shielded and protected in the calm
Of Fortalice, Bolton's haven, free from malice.

Urban Outreach

Wandering, community missionaries seek out
The homeless and destitute all about,
To house and feed them very well,
Delivering them from evil and their hell,
So that they can survive and tell
Of the day they were saved from the street,
By Bolton's Urban Outreach on the beat,
Furiously working at full steam.
A wonderful, ubiquitous team.

Key Workers, Carers, NHS, Volunteers

You are the ones...Being first to quench our thirst.
You are the ones...Taking us out and about.
You are the ones...Helping the poor to endure.
You are the ones...Cleansing our need when we bleed.
You are the ones...Making us survive and be alive.
Where would we be if you were not there?
For you really are the ones who actually care!

Bolton Magnetism

For over 50 years you've been our home,
Never the urge to leave or roam
To the allure of the North or South.
Upbeat, empowered, never down in the mouth.
We were attracted by opportunity being a reality
In Bolton's outstanding Municipality.
Full of love and wonderful hospitality.
May it for ever and ever be
Home for you and for me.

Dig Deep, Give Kindly

Delighted to involve you in our quest
For the gradely folk of Bolton to invest,
In volunteers, charities and community ways
Of giving Bolton life even better days.
So put hands in your pockets and dig deep
Increasing our funds so the needy can reap,
The rewards of the Mayor's Charity Chest
And the gradely folk of Bolton be heaven blessed!

The Challenge: A Poem a Day

Never mind an apple a day!
It's a poem a day
That keeps the doctor away!
This you'll find
Stimulates the body and your mind.
Poetry nurtures and expresses in advance
Emotions and feelings not just by chance,
But by a calculating, literary stance.
A poem you'll find,
Generates the body and a thoughtful mind,
To lead from the front and not behind.
This helps to foster lively hospitality
To raise Charitable funds in reality,
Very much appreciated by the Mayoralty.
So you will find,
A poem a day,
Keeps you healthy, wealthy
In your body and your mind.

Come into the Parlour Soon

Hope to see you in the Parlour for a do.
After Lockdown, social distance, don't forget.
Difficult times to say the least,
With COVID-19 the evil beast.
The Mayor will do her best, Heaven blessed!
To welcome you to the new normal, less formal.
Hope to see you then one and all,
At the Mayor's Great Annual Ball.

Appreciation for All You Do

Clap, clap, wherever you may be
For the NHS and carers in our community.
Applaud, applaud as loud as you can
For those saving lives...a special clan.
Thursdays should always be
For the NHS, Carers and Key workers
Out there in our humble Community
So clap, clap wherever you be!

Please Invite Us when You Can

No function, no event too big or small,
The Mayor and Consort will attend all.
Delighted to promote, this wide, varied range
No matter how outlandish or strange.
So invite us, do not hesitate and hide,
You Firms and Businesses Borough wide,
Schools, Voluntary, Charitable and Cultural hubs
Local amenities, Churches and Sports Clubs.
Special Guests, individual residents too,
It would be wonderful for us to see you!
We'll let you know when we're out of Lockdown
And can freely move about the Town.
Contact us by email: *mayorsoffice@bolton.gov.uk*
Or telephone 01204 331090 the Office on any day.

Bn Simply the Best

The Bolton News,
Always shares wonderful views
Of the newly elected Mayor.
You are great for being there
Showing that you really care.
Please cover us again and again,
We don't know where, we don't know when,
But until then,
Thanks for just being there,
You are simply the Best!

Bolton FM...Spread, Spread the Word

Bolton FM the Radio Station
Supports the Mayoralty with elation,
Promoting each and every cause
With appreciation and applause.
For a little while we're not about
So get our message out
Support our Charities far and wide,
You generous listeners locked safely inside!

First External Engagement

An excursion to the flamboyant Queen's Park,
In the bright daytime, not in the gloomy dark.
Could not have arrived a minute too soon,
During this lovely, splendid month of June.
Only a photographer and a few people there,
It was a silent, thoughtful, solitary affair.
Since becoming Mayor I've waited hours,
To witness my name crafted in colourful flowers.
Making this first rendezvous as Mayor
Has made me and my team quite aware,
That COVID-19 heralds exceptional days
For the Mayoralty in many different ways.

Covid-19 Denies the Mayoral Procession

This year, there is no Mayoral Procession,
We have to accept this COVID confession.
To the Parish Church, there'll be no walk
No prayers and blessings nor talk the talk
There will be a virtual acceptance vote,
Take heed and make an attentive note
Of there being nothing auspicious too
Much obliged and a very special thank you.

Suspended Animation?

Bolton just like the whole Nation
Hangs in suspended Animation,
With many in self isolation.
As COVID-19 forever soars
Little movement, no Leisure Tours
Doing a lot more at home, indoors.
Going to watch the Wanderers, we miss
But we will not sink into the abyss,
Just hold our heads high in bliss
As Bolton like the whole Nation
Is in suspended animation,
Until we are out from splendid isolation.

Is This the Real World?

Locked in virtual reality,
No engagements for the Mayoralty.
Miss you ever so much!
Please keep us in touch.
Highlight the times to be had
By mobile, laptop or iPad.
Wave through windows to us inside.
Keep us in touch, do not hide!
Post Pandemic heralds a new Municipality,
Outside and not in virtual reality.
Hopefully giving us some vanity
Devoid during this COVID insanity.

Do as You Are Told

Makes you cough and wheeze, the coronavirus disease.
Do not be bold, do as you are told!
Do not roam, stay at home!
It eliminates your taste with haste.
Do not be bold, do as you are told!
Do not roam, stay at home!
It destroys your sense of smell as well.
Do not be bold, do as you are told!
Stay at home, wash your hands, save lives!

Homeless

Lying in the shop doorway last night,
Alone in the dark and out of sight.
You were snug in a cardboard box,
Shoeless and just wearing socks.
To you someone came and spoke,
A concerned lady and a bloke.
They gave you some food and a hot drink,
And took you to a shelter, I think?

Time and Tide

Seconds, minutes, hours seem to mime
Take it just a day at a time.
Days, months, years seem to go
But time and tide flow.
Feels like centuries, even a millennium
Since this COVID-19 era come.
We know it is but a drop in the ocean,
But wow! What a violent commotion.

Poetic Muse

During Lockdown, Isolation, and Shielded indoors,
I put Poetry in motion as I did my chores.
Ideas and feelings blossomed from my inspired mind.
A literary pleasure and not a monotonous grind.
As I composed a poem, verse and rhyme
Poetic licence and creation occupied my time.
The flow of words seemed so clear and fine
Taking a well-earned place line by line.
The Poetic Muse embraced and enveloped time
As I composed a poem, verse and rhyme.

The Silent Assassin

See no evil, hear no evil, speak no evil,
But watch out! COVID -19 is out there!
The silent Assassin permeates everywhere.
Words and deeds will fail to kill,
But coronavirus will!
Never let your guard down!
Do not frolic in town!
Beware the silent assassin
Is just passing!

The Octagon Phoenix Arises

You must all rally round and totally agree
That local theatre is where we want to be,
To see scintillating performance and exceptional drama
In the new Octagon amidst its vista and panorama!
No one quite knows when...God forbid!
Where thespians will be after this wretched COVID.
Patrons and enthusiasts wait with bated breath,
To ensure that theatre will not suffer corona death.

The Octagon Really Needs You

Become a Stage Guardian Angel PATRON,
Save the magic of local theatre,
As you become a real wealth creator
For the renowned OCTAGON THEATRE.
Whether it be twenty, forty or a hundred pounds,
There are no monetary limits nor bounds.
Invest now and join this influential group,
Keeping theatre goers in the Bolton loop.

Keep Upto Date

A COVID-19 BULLETIN broadcast on the TV
Gave the latest information for you and me.
Stay at home, stay alert and keep your nerve
Graphs are showing the diminishing curve,
Reduced bus, rail and car travel,
The facts and their effects unravel
Indicating statistics and everything said
About COVID-19 and the many dead.

Historical Repetition

The 14th century saw the BLACK DEATH
Killing thousands of villagers in depth.
The 17th century saw the GREAT PLAGUE
Wiping out thousands of young and old age.
Then, England's population was small.
Now there are 66 million people in all.
There have been other diseases all told,
But none quite like COVID-19 so bold.
The future will tell of this PANDEMIC,
The life blood of historians and the ACADEMIC.
Like no other disease it has no equal,
Let's hope too, there is no sequel!
Children will ask many a question and more
"Grandad what did you do in the CORONA war?"
"I self-isolated and shielded behind our door".
Except on Thursdays when I led the applause
For those who did so much for the survival cause...
Nurses, Doctors, Key and Care Workers galore,
Volunteers, family, friends and many more.

The Invisible Marauder

From now on you will permeate all that we do
Incessant marauding all the day through.
We will test, track and contact trace
Checking COVID velocity, spread and pace.
Vigilance and caution will always be there,
Catch us if you can or even dare!
Some day there will be the inevitable end
To this virus that sent us round the bend.
We fought you and we kept our nerve,
We lowered the infection rate to flatten the curve.
It makes us all house bound prisoners alike,
Take great care for lest we see another spike!
We must continue testing, tracing and tracking,
Determined and there must not be any slacking,
Until the cities, towns and villages are all rid
Of this fatal, invisible and evil marauder...COVID.

We Live in Hope

Bolton take a deep breath
And count to ten,
We're in COVID's depth
But then,
We are diminishing the peak
Over mountain and glen
Too soon to speak
Lest it will rise again!
Hopefully no longer to be seen
After a possible vaccine
Dominates the scene
But then....
Who knows?
As it comes and goes?

Not yet Homeward Bound

In many a town the numbers are down.
This is so great to see; I think you'll agree.
Take care, beware COVID is still around
Not quite yet HOMEWARD BOUND!

How the Times Have Changed

There has never been
So many domestic gardeners or cooks.
We have never seen
The reading of so many books.
Times are rather lean
Home shielding in Lockdown.
We see the garden green
In much of the Town.
There is something in between
Listening to the radio and watching TV
Confined to the silver screen
Devouring boxsets in a wild spree.
This is how it's been,
A way of life seldom seen,
COVID has a lot to answer for,
Will there be a normal anymore?
We will see one day
But there will be a long delay.

Post Pandemic

No one knows how the COVID era will pan out?
Conjecture, wonder and much to talk about.
Will those halcyon days ever return?
Are there still many lessons to learn?
We are thinking of the better days,
Perhaps work and travel in different ways?
Will we work at home and have a 4-day week?
Will manufacturing be given a tweak?
There are many questions we need to ask,
About social distancing and wearing a mask?
No one really can answer our concern,
So long as we live, forgive and learn!

Silently Ponder

Remember tenderly those we lost
As we gently count the COVID cost.
Pray for those we no longer see
Long may their cherished memories be.
It is a tragedy that so many died,
Painful memories for families who survived.

Progress but Still on Message

A new way of life is testing and tracing
Together with continuous 2 metre pacing.
We are lifting slowly Lockdown restrictions,
Reducing hinderances and conflictions.
Some remark it has not come too soon
Afterall we are in the month of June.
If we obey there will be little concern,
But if we are careless restrictions will return.
Shielded people will continue mainly inside,
Little has changed so they must abide
By following the coronavirus rules,
Stay home, be healthy and wise not fools!

"Brave New World"

There's a new way of teaching in our schools.
There's a new way of preaching not breaking the rules.
Things are returning as a small measure,
But take care value your life as a pleasure.
Everyone especially children wash your hands,
Surfaces retain this virus where it lands.

Move with Caution!

There appears to be more traffic in our street,
Where socially distanced people seem to meet.
The month of May has now passed
And Lockdown eased for many at last.
But make sure you still take care,
Out and about socialising everywhere.
COVID-19 has not gone away,
Sorry folks it is still here today!

Nice to Have Some Fresh Air

Exercise and meet in the park but hark!
Rendezvous in your street 2 metres apart...7 feet.
This is your right, in the daytime or at night.
Walk, run or use your bike, do anything you like.
Appreciate being out there, in the fresh air.
But still socially distance and take extra care.

Just Be Positive

Years, a type 2 diabetic, a rheumatoid, osteo arthritic,
Having hyper-tension and now drawing my pension.
Suffered many a DVT, failing kidneys at CKd 3.
Then hospitalised with sepsis but survived this.
I rise from bed each day, raring to go and play.
Now I have a dodgy prostate, illness seems fate.
Many like this in our Nation, yet full of inspiration.
Not just to survive but to prosper and thrive
And yes! Dedicated to the NHS, wonderful God Bless!

What a Tragedy!

It seems ages now since this deadly virus started.
It was such a tragedy when you all departed.
You have left us all in tears and broken hearted.
Family could not be there as you took your last breath.
We could not hold your hand before your death.
It is such an enormous, devastating, tragic crime
That COVID took your life well before your time!

The Prowler

Do not be a night owl, coronavirus is on the prowl.
Feels and searches in the dark, as happy as a skylark.
It probes and seeks; it gropes and sneaks
In wardrobes upstairs where it clings and stares
To surprise you and catch you unawares.
It is evil in thought and deed as it satisfies its greed.
When it unwraps your untimely, predictable fate,
Watch out, stay safe, remain alert my precious mate.
Protect all in the family nest avoid the prowler at best.

Easing Lockdown

We still can't muster in a crowd.
Staying side by side is not allowed.
There will be no mass celebrations
Or family reunions with all your relations.
We can liaise with at least one friend.
All this is for the best in the end.
Hopefully little by little we'll return to normal
With lots of Hugging and being less formal.

Schools, Stores, Delivery Drivers, Posties

Providing homework and activities galore,
Heads and their teachers can do no more.
They cater for vulnerable, special needs,
Giving children education and their feeds,
At home and some at school,
This has happened continuously as a rule.
Posties still deliver letters in our street
Waving through windows to all they greet.
So pleased that you' re keeping us in touch,
Ever grateful and thank you so much.
Shops and their delivery drivers have kept us fed.
Giving us so many excuses to get out of bed.
Providing and selling food in our stores,
Bringing and leaving provisions at our doors.
Family, volunteers have been at our beck and call
We are really indebted to you one and all.

"Only the Air that We Breathe"

Fewer buses and trains, not many cars nor planes.
Diminished emissions out there, less contaminated air.
Walking, cycling, running the norm CO_2 out of form
At levels seldom seen for ages...where have you been?
We can intoxicate fresh air with fewer emissions there.
Stay 2 metres apart and do it with all your heart.
Wash your hands, be alert the air is full of less dirt.
Inhale, take deep breaths and avoid COVID deaths.
It would be absolute bliss if the air stays like this.

"But for the Grace of God"

Not vulnerable nor low, for the grace of God we go.
Not all free of plight, some have a sleepless night.
Dependent upon volunteers I guess like the CVS.
In rain, snow or sleet, always there for you to meet
In times of need and loss or you want a bed to doss.
Fit for the daily plod, go I, but for the "grace of God"

Still Smile, Even though...

Stay home, stay safe but smile,
Even for just a little while'
Diseased from head to toe,
Remain hopeful and raring to go!
Pleased to wake up and be alive
Not just existing but ready to thrive!
Glad that you are here too,
Helping each other all day through!
Fortunate to have the supportive clan,
Providing for every woman, child and man!
Sound in spirit, body and mind
Even though you may be wrinkled and lined!
Panic not! It is just for a while,
Stay home, stay safe but smile!

You Will Never Win

Lockdown, isolated and shielded
Will never smash our spirit wielded!
It brightens the mind, sharpens our power,
Making life better hour by hour!
Be aware unseen transmitter!
You make us determined if not bitter
To keep your evil at bay,
Improving the world each day
We will fight and never give in,
COVID-19 you will never win!

Happy to Be with You

We see couples throughout the Nation
Closer together in lockdown and self-isolation.
Loving being indoors, improving what we do.
It is great and I love being just with you.
Basking in our May sunshine garden
Is a well-earned, welcomed pardon!
From that dangerous world outside,
Where tragically, many have not survived.

Friendly Caring Bolton

Since time begun so much has been done,
For the many by the few, without further ado.
Bolton toasts people who serve with eternal verve,
Those needing a hand from those who understand.
Providing in thought and deed for individual need
In all walks of life, disabled, infirm or abused wife.
Supporting the community by resources raised in unity,
Bolton is the place to be, the kindest town you'll see,
Caring for young and old, with special hearts of gold.
Bolton is where to be, for friendship and its Majesty.

On Your Bike!

Get those wheels turning,
Take exercise but be discerning!
Stay alert and keep your distance
As portrayed with Government insistence.
Fantastic going for a bike ride,
So much better than being locked inside!

Enough's Enough, Please Go!

You're wider than the ocean,
Much deeper than the sea,
COVID, when will you let us be?
You're taller than the Mountains,
Denser than the Dead sea,
COVID, when will you let us be?
You're greater than life itself,
Surpassing God's everlasting mercy,
COVID, when will you let us be?
Your strike rate is diminishing,
Are you now finishing?
Or is there another uproar?
COVID, let us be!
Cannot take ANYMORE!

Missing You Lots

All ten of our grandchildren we miss,
Seeing and cuddling them would be bliss.
Yet virtual contact does not go amiss.
Warm hugs are so much better than this.
Coronavirus has made us well aware,
That at a distance you are all there.
We cannot touch but give a smile and stare,
For those we love so much and care.

Save the Economy, Open Your School

As a retired Secondary Head,
It is hard to say that it would be wise
For Schools to return with reduced class size!
R levels below 1 is how we are led,
Everyone's safety is the duty of the Head.
So glad I am retired, enough said!
An immense decision for body and soul,
Relieved that I no longer have that role!

Don't Blame Covid for Everything

April, May and June blessed with fantastic heat,
As I water flowers, bushes from my garden seat.
Each plant seems to replenish in sheer relief.
Me too, for survival is our ultimate belief.
Soon there may well be a hose pipe ban,
So get that garden done as fast as you can!
In a while there's going to be rationed water,
So save those flowers and bushes from slaughter.
As you contemplate from that garden seat,
Remember it is not COVID but the intense heat.

Still Given the Daily Dose

Given Lockdown and shielded as a daily dose
Has not made me down hearted nor morose.
It's a medicinal treatment to be obeyed,
That's the honest truth I'm afraid!
So wander not! Wash your hands! Don't stray!
Socially distanced apart and out of harm's way,
And you will get to live yet another day!
Lockdown medicine keeps me alive and I thrive!

The Covid Economy

So much for us to debit, furlough or Universal Credit
Mortgage breaks made; Utility Bills delayed.
80% wages, Loans enjoyed, including the Self Employed
From bottom to top, the COVID Economy shows a drop
In manufacturing growth and GDP, such a calamity!
Funding to ease the pain, Government taking the strain
There's no transgression as we slip into recession.

Six Pack, Ok!

Alone, writing yet another poem in the sun,
Is not something so special for every single one.
In fact, it is a therapeutic hobby for the few,
The many wait for freedom, long overdue!
They remain shackled inside without any chains,
Anxiously hopeful for restriction lifting gains.
At last, we can meet family members and six others
But alas, we still can't hug and kiss our mothers.
Stay socially distanced out in the crowd everyone!
By the way. The Celtic Bard is writing alone in the sun.

Uncertain

June the first has quenched my thirst,
There's now a glimmer of light and delight,
We may have the grand children in sight.
True with hand on heart, that's a start.
It is a fact, that we can have social contact.
But I am not so sure, about this dubious allure?

Chewing the Fat

Neighbours spoke to us over the fence today.
First time for ages and had much to say.
And we kept our distance 2 metres away.
It was a pleasure to have had a brief chat,
In the sunshine from where we sat
So important a discussion was that.
Socially distanced at 2 metres away,
Neighbours spoke to us over the fence today.

Hope on the Horizon

There is real hope on the Horizon,
Be sure not to throw it all away.
Just take those phased steps
From now and every other day.
There is real hope on the Horizon
As we slowly emerge from strict Lockdown,
Taking those phased steps,
As daily life returns ever so softly in Town.
There is real hope on the Horizon,
Err on the delicate side of caution, be aware,
We have only flattened the curve,
Just take gentle steps, COVID is still there.

SW19

No Wimbledon Tennis this June,
Safe practice begins very soon,
But the thrilling, excitement at SW19
For now has come and been.
Thousands not living this Grand Slam dream,
Nor eating those scrumptious strawberries and cream!

Behind Closed Doors

Premiership footballers have been back training,
Given the go ahead after much complaining!
There will be some friendly matches,
Behind closed doors so no one catches
The coronavirus and hence:
The Premier League will recommence
With team players staying in their bubble,
Being safe and out of dreadful trouble.
You may not all agree, however, we will see
Televised games behind the closed door
Hoping that the COVID-19 curve does not soar!

Paderborn and Le Mans

No LIBORI, no Twinning Visit this July,
We cannot go by Rail, Sea nor Fly!
Le Mans and Paderborn to make amends
Sent best wishes to we, their friends.
"Die besten wunsche, Meilleurs voeux"
Hope to come and see you next year!

Not Just Covid Depression

Anxiety, panic attacks and feeling low,
Have made some hapless not raring to go.
The COVID pandemic has frozen the brain
Sending affected ones quite insane.
Make sure you stay alert and smart,
By talking to someone or doing some art;
That would be positive from the start.
Occupy your time with things to do,
This will be much needed therapy for you.
Remember if you feel isolated and alone
There is always someone else at the end of the phone.
Anxiety, panic attacks and feeling low
Speak to someone, try to go with the flow.
Much help is around out there,
From trained, concerned individuals who care.
Do not suffer in silence or be alone,
Make the effort, arise and pick up the phone.

Sporting Hiatus

No British Open at the Seaside Links
Until the coronavirus is over, me thinks.
No Derby horse racing at Epsom
These are the rules, so accept them.
No spectators inside Football Stadia allowed
Remember two is company and three is a crowd.
No Grand Prix meetings in the mix,
You will not see cricketers hit a six.
No Tennis Stars on centre court,
No Rugby competitions of any sort,
It is a tremendous nightmare for competitive sport.

75 Years Celebration

In 1945, Victory in Europe was achieved,
Everyone at home was so relieved.
On May 8th we celebrated 75 years of Peace,
Momentarily we allowed Lockdown to cease
As we partied on the drive at our front door
The end of the Second World War.
Neighbours remained on their own driveway,
Dancing, singing to the music of a bygone day.
Gracie Fields, Flanagan and Allen, Dame Vera Lynn,
Pierced the Old Vicarage air and all therein.
We decorated the garage in red, white and blue,
Dressed up in period costume all day through.
We ate sandwiches and had homemade cakes,
Singing war songs with all that it takes
Socially distanced and staying 2 metres apart,
We celebrated VE day with all of our Heart!

Airways Blocked Conundrum

Ironic though it appears to be,
COVID affects our airways you see.
Whether it be Respiratory System or Airports,
COVID has caused havoc of all sorts.
Heathrow, Gatwick, Manchester and the likes
Have been hit because of COVID strikes.
British Airways, Virgin Atlantic and many more
Have grounded their planes on the floor.
It is so ironic that COVID has blocked most flying,
And locked us indoors to stop us dying.
Our airways are the lifeline of our economy.
Our airways are the lifeline of our body!
Ironic though it appears to be
COVID affects our airways in parity.

Mother's and Father's Day what Will Be?

No Easter parades and no Whit Walks',
Just from a distance measured talks.
Easter Bonnets there were quite a few,
But not so many appeared in view.
Easter and Whit Sunday came and went,
Without much celebration but with intent.
Mothering Sunday and Father's Day took place,
But there were no family visitors in your face.
There were plenty of cards and beautiful flowers,
But the whole occasion did not last hours.
There was the distant wave and that happy shout,
Yet none of this would knock you out,
Will there ever be more Easter Parades and Whit walks
Or will it remain the same, distanced, measured talks?

Volunteer Work, a Classic, Premier Return

From the first to the sixth of June,
Indeed, this was not a minute too soon!
We acknowledged 'National Volunteer Week',
A tremendous accolade so to speak.
We then saw the Classic 2000 Guineas Horse Race,
And heard the Epsom Derby will also take place.
To crown it all the decision was surprisingly taken,
To finish the Premier League, if I'm not mistaken?
It is true that social distancing will still prevail
And the price of safety is not for sale,
As sport returns in a somewhat sterile atmosphere,
Who knows if there's a price to pay so dear.

Postscript

These poems were composed between March and June 2020. They are dedicated to families who face many trials and tribulations, ups and downs in this dreadful, historic COVID-19 period. They portray happier moments, the comfort and support of family, friends, key workers and volunteers. They illuminate and put into perspective what really matters in life; life itself. I apologise if anyone feels hurt or uncomfortable by any of these poems. They are subjective and accurate historically for the current period of coronavirus pandemic and are not intended to be political given the neutrality of the Mayoralty.

"The Mayor has awarded 500+ Certificates of Recognition to Bolton people, organisations, businesses, volunteers and charities who have gone that extra mile to support their communities during the pandemic".

Certificate
of recognition

This certificate is to recognise the wonderful work you have done to save lives, keep people safe and stop the spread of Covid-19.

On behalf of the people of Bolton I thank you for your selflessness, commitment and sheer determination to go above and beyond in this crisis.

I commend you and offer my heartfelt appreciation and gratitude for everything you have done.

Your work now and in the future will benefit generations to come and will not be forgotten.

With best wishes

Linda Thomas

Mayor of Bolton
Councillor Linda Thomas
June 2020

Food for Thought

Staying healthy in body and mind has been the focus during this unprecedented COVID pandemic and lockdown restrictions. Writing poems became my food for thought and eating tasty food stimulated the poetic juices. This gave me the sustenance and inspiration, not only to survive, but to be creative both mentally and physically. Creating three good meals a day was just as an imaginative task as composing three good poems a day.

With food in mind, the Mayor and I thought about the well-established Bolton Food and Drink Festival and how this year, as have many other events, it became virtual. We approached the successful Bolton chef Michael Harrison and asked if he and his fellow gourmet friends would contribute recipes. The result is a collection of delicious meals that anyone can make in their own home; and will get anyone through future lockdowns.

Pandemic Poems, Mayoralty,
The Perfect Recipe
And all for charity!

Recipes

Starters

Curried carrot soup *by Michael Caines*
Crumpets *by Mike Harrison*
Black pudding scotch egg *by The Cherry Tree*
Spicy lamb sausage roll *by Sushma Solanki*
Sticky chicken thighs *by Mike Harrison*
Lancashire tart *by Tom Bridge*
Hogweed floret cheese *by Colin Unsworth*
Thai Noodles *by Matt Carr*

Mains

Tuna Nicoise *by Nicholas Cullen*
Beer braised brisket *by Northern Monkey*
Cheese and onion pie *by Scott Bannon*
Beef pot roast *by Simon Wood*
Mughlai Kadhai Paneer *by Kishan Shah*
Balti burger and roast potato wedges *by Anjali Pathak*
Cod loin tacos *by Mike Harrison*

Desserts

Coffee and walnut cake with cheesecake filling *by Jackie Heaton*
Biscoff tiramisu *by Gareth Mason*
The best ever chocolate fudge cake *by Natasha Lees*
Apple tart Tain *by Jean Christophe Novelli*
Vimto trifle *by Robert Owen Brown*

Curried carrot soup

SERVES 4

INGREDIENTS

150g onions, chopped

2 cloves of garlic, peeled
and lightly crushed

500g carrots, peeled and
chopped small

150g unsalted butter

1 teaspoon cumin seeds

a large pinch of Madras
curry powder

300ml chicken stock

500ml water

1 bouquet garni (parsley
stalks, coriander stalks,
thyme, bay leaf, celery
and leek, tied with
string)

fresh coriander leaves

METHOD

1   Cook the onion, garlic and carrots gently in a saucepan
    with a pinch of salt with the butter, without colouring,
    for 5 minutes.

2   Meanwhile, toast the cumin seeds in a dry pan. Add
    the toasted cumin and Madras curry powder to the
    vegetables and cook for a further 2 minutes, then add
    the chicken stock, water and bouquet garni. Bring to the
    boil and add a little salt, then reduce to a simmer and
    leave to cook slowly for 30 minutes.

3   Transfer to a blender and blend to a fine purée, then
    pass the purée through a sieve and return it to a clean
    pan. Check the seasoning and serve sprinkled with
    freshly chopped coriander leaves.

Michael Caines MBE DL
www.lympstonemanor.co.uk

Crumpets

SERVES 4

INGREDIENTS

1 tsp sugar
200ml whole milk
100ml warm water
1tbsp dried yeast
150g strong white flour
100g plain flour
1 tsp salt
½ tsp bicarbonate of soda
20g butter, for cooking

METHOD

1   Mix the sugar, milk and warm water in a jug and stir in the yeast. Leave in a warm place for 15 minutes until frothy.

2   Combine the flours in a large mixing bowl with the salt. Stir in the liquid and mix vigorously until smooth. Cover and leave in a warm place for between one-and-a-half and two hours until the batter is a mass of tiny bubbles.

3   Mix the bicarbonate of soda with 50ml warm water and stir it into the batter. Cover and leave in a warm place for 30 minutes.

4   Melt the butter and use it to brush the inside of four crumpet rings. Heat a large frying pan on a medium-low heat and grease the pan. Put the rings flat into the pan and ladle a spoonful of batter into each, so they are about half full.

5   Cook until the top is dry and festooned with holes, then push the crumpets out of the rings (you may need a knife for this operation). If eating immediately, toast the tops under a hot grill until golden, then serve. If you're keeping them, cool on a wire rack, then toast on both sides to reheat.

6   Great topped with Southport seafoods, potted shrimps & a little rocket.

Mike Harrison
www.cheftogo.co.uk

Black pudding scotch egg

INGREDIENTS

4 x eggs
200g flour
200g breadcrumbs
*200ml of milk mixed
   with 2 eggs*
240g of black pudding
200g sausage meat
2 shallots fine diced
*1 garlic clove finely
   chopped*

METHOD

1 Place a pan on the stove with water in to boil

2 Cook the eggs in the water for 6 minutes for a medium egg and 7 minutes for large then place into ice water to stop the cooking

3 Peel the shell from the eggs and set aside in the fridge

4 Cook the shallot and garlic in a pan till soft then leave too cool

5 Mix the black pudding on a mixer with the paddle until broken down and soft. Then add sausage meat and shallot mix add salt and pepper and fry a small piece off to check seasoning.

6 Wet your hands in warm water then Ball 40g of the black pudding. Then press the mix out flat.

7 Place the egg in the centre of the mix and gently wrap the egg in the black pudding mix until it's completely covered.

8 Roll in flour then the milk and egg mix and then into the breadcrumbs too, coat then again set in the fridge.

9 Cook in a fryer until golden brown then place in an oven on 180c for 6 Minutes.

10 We serve ours with an apple gel, celeriac remoulade and dried Parma ham crisps.

The Cherry Tree, Blackrod
www.cherrytreeblackrod.com

Homemade spicy lamb sausage rolls

MAKES 12

INGREDIENTS

Olive oil

1 red onion, peeled and
   finely chopped

1 clove garlic, peeled and
   crushed

1 ½ tsp Garam masala

½ tsp red chilli powder

½ tsp Turmeric

500g lamb mince

Small bunch coriander,
   finely chopped

2 sheets ready-rolled puff
   pastry

1 egg, beaten Sea salt
   flakes Black and white
   sesame seeds

METHOD

1   Heat a splash of oil in a frying pan, add the onion and
    garlic and fry gently for 3-4 minutes until softened. Add
    the spices and cook for another 30-40 seconds. Tip into
    a bowl and leave to cool.

2   Once cooled add to lamb mince stir to combine. Add the
    coriander and mix thoroughly, seasoning with a good
    pinch of salt.

3   Take half of the mixture and form it into a sausage
    shape along the long side of one of the sheets of puff
    pastry. Roll up the pastry to seal in the filling then
    trim the excess pastry, making sure the seam is on the
    underside of the sausage roll. Repeat with the remaining
    filling and pastry.

4   Brush the sausage rolls with the beaten egg and sprinkle
    over the sesame seeds and a pinch of salt. Cut each large
    roll into 6 then transfer to a lined baking tray and chill
    for an hour.

5   Preheat the oven to 200ºC. Bake the sausage rolls for
    25-30 minutes until cooked through. Leave to cool
    slightly before serving.

Sushma Solanki
www.sushmasnacks.weebly.com

Sticky citrus chicken thighs

INGREDIENTS

*2 jaffa oranges, 1 juiced,
    1 thickly sliced*
3 tbsp maple syrup
2 tbsp olive oil
2 tbsp sherry vinegar
*1 tbsp wholegrain
    mustard*
4 chicken thighs, skin on
*140g small shallots, left
    whole but peeled*
*2 thyme sprigs, broken
    up a bit*
1 tsp sesame seeds

METHOD

1   Heat oven to 180°C/160°C fan/gas 4. Juice 1 of the oranges
    and whisk together with the maple syrup, olive oil,
    vinegar, mustard and redcurrant jelly.

2   Place the chicken thighs and shallots in a roasting tray.
    Drizzle over half the orange sauce with some seasoning
    and toss to coat everything. Roast for 40 mins.

3   Remove the tin from the oven and put the orange
    slices in among the chicken. Scatter over the thyme
    and drizzle over the rest of the orange sauce. Roast for
    another 15 mins until the chicken is tender and cooked
    through, and everything is sticky and golden.

4   Mix in the sesame seeds and cook for another 5 mins.
    Serve straight away, remembering to scrape out all the
    sticky juices from the tin, and eat with wilted spinach,
    plus a little rice to soak up the sauce.

Mike Harrison
Twitter @cheftogo

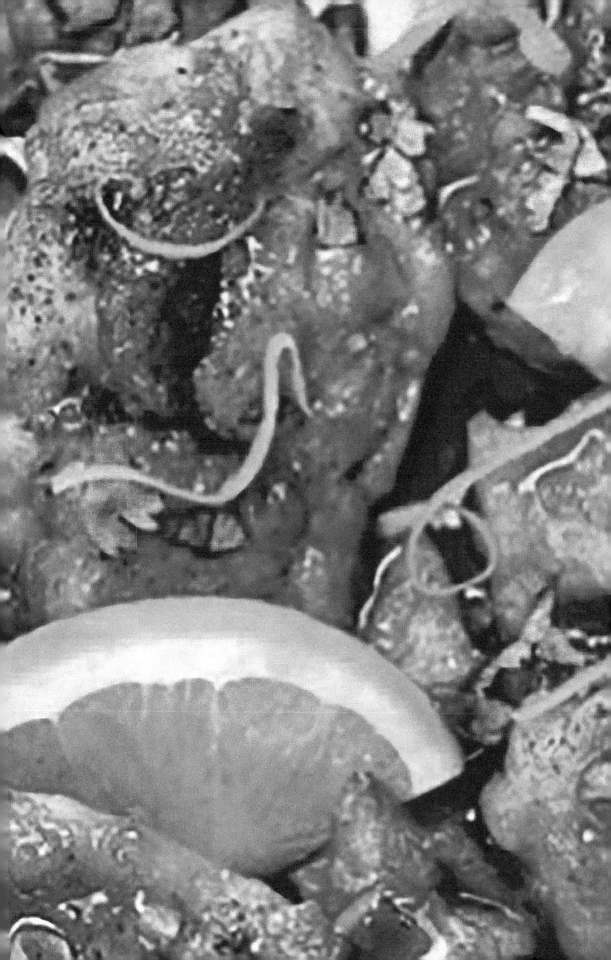

Lancashire tart

INGREDIENTS

1 blind-baked (baked with no filling beforehand) shortcrust base

1 large removable bottomed flan tin /case

900 ml jug of Lancashire cheese sauce

100g/4oz Black Pudding

100g/4oz Crispy Bacon

100g/4oz Cooked Potato

100g/4oz Sausage meat (95% pure pork)

1 mini egg omelette

Lancashire cheese

METHOD

1 Preheat the oven to 140°C/275°F/Gas mark 1 to 2.

2 Starting with 1 layer of Black pudding in a round disc shape and top with 100ml of cheese sauce.

3 Add 1 layer of Crispy Bacon and top with 100ml of cheese sauce.

4 Add 1 layer of cooked, thinly sliced potato and top with 100ml of cheese sauce.

5 Add 1 layer of sausage meat and top with 100ml of cheese sauce.

6 Add the mini egg omelette and top with 100ml of cheese sauce.

7 Finish with another layer of sliced potatoes with at least 1-inch topping of crumbly Lancashire cheese, topped with the cheese sauce.

8 Bake in a low oven for 40 minutes until the liquid is set. Allow to cool, cover with cling film, and place a heavy fitting plate with a weight on top to compress the layers.

(c) Tom Bridge.

Taken from the cookbook, PIE SOCIETY.

Hogweed floret cheese

A great alternative to cauliflower cheese

SERVES APPROX. 6

INGREDIENTS

Hogweed florets
50g butter
50g plain flour
50g grated cheese
1 pint milk
Salt/pepper

METHOD

1   Wash the florets to remove any insects, par boil for 3 mins.

2   Melt the butter in a saucepan and remove from the heat.

3   Add the flour salt and pepper and stir well until you get a smooth paste, return to the heat and gently fry for a couple of minutes then remove from the heat again.

4   Slowly add the milk, stirring all the time to prevent lumps, return to the hob, add 30g of the cheese and cook while stirring until the sauce thickens.

5   Stir in the hogweed florets and place in an oven proof dish, sprinkle the rest of the cheese on top and bake in the oven at 200°C/400°F or Gas mark 6 for 30 mins or until the top is golden brown.

Colin Unsworth
www.foresthorizons.co.uk

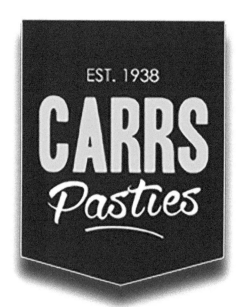

EST. 1938

CARRS
Pasties

My brother Liam, like our dad before him, can often be found in the kitchen of our factory, preparing food treats for the hardworking folks that are responsible for making the humble Carrs Pasty. Buffalo wings are a particular favourite.

Mike Harrison himself has also occasionally been spotted, creating twists on our whist pies amongst other creations. We don't pay him or anything, he just turns up, lovely man that he is.

So when asked to submit a recipe for this book, my thoughts turned to the fact that I really should get involved with the bakery treat concept and put together a dish that will keep our pasty people satisfied for the rest of the shift. Of course this works for a party of 10 or 5, altering the amounts as you go.

Credit to Nigel Slater for providing the original recipe that started me off on the "Hot Sweet Salt Sour" journey of noodle dishes that I have been feeding guests in our home for many years and now has been scaled up for Team Carr. The main thing about this dish is that it is just a big playground to have fun in, there is no wrong way of going about it.

Matt Carr

Thai Noodles

INGREDIENTS

Small handful of coriander seeds, at least 40, roasted lightly in a frying pan before grinding

1 tbsp turmeric

2 large bunches of fresh coriander, chopped

1 big piece of ginger, peeled and sliced into matchsticks.

6 Thai green chillies, chopped and seeded

1 whole bulb of garlic, cloves peeled and sliced.

½ bottle of Nam Pla (salty fish sauce)

Groundnut oil for high heat cooking

4 lemongrass sticks (outer hard bits removed) finely chopped (best ground with the coriander seeds)

10 chicken thighs, skin on,

10 chicken drumsticks, skin on

10 chicken wings

5 carrots, peeled and chopped into sticks of the same size

3 broccoli heads divided into florets with the lighter green parts chopped away and the stalks chopped into the same sized sticks as the carrots

6 Bell peppers or any large peppers that you prefer, roughly chopped

2 bunches of spring onions (finely chopped green leaf bits and keep separate)

2 tins of coconut milk

6 fresh limes

2 tbsp sugar

10 nests of medium egg noodles (or any type you like)

METHOD

1 Heat oven to 220°C. Salt the chicken pieces in roasting trays, drizzle a little oil over them and roast until cooked.

   Set aside and once cooled, remove the meat and chop into bite sized chunks, store in a bowl for later.

2 Put the wings and remaining bones and skin in a big pot, add enough boiling water to cover them and boil at a medium to high heat, (this will bring out the flavour of the chicken into the liquid and produce a chicken stock).

3 Reduce the liquid until only a little is left and the bones start to sizzle in the pot to bring out a more intense flavour - add some more boiling water at the end which reconstitutes the stock liquid.

4 Add the ground toasted coriander seeds, lemongrass, chillies, ginger, garlic, turmeric, chopped coriander in a big bowl and mix together before adding to a wok or large pot, on high heat with a little oil.

5 Keep everything moving as the paste fries and the flavours combine. Once the kitchen is full of the smell of fried paste, add the coconut milk and when ready, the chicken stock.

6 This soupy liquid is the base for the dish. Keep it simmering and keep an eye on the thickness. If it's too watery, cook it down a little.

7 Add nam pla, sugar and lime juice. Now then - this dish succeeds or fails on achieving a balance of spice heat, salt, sour and sweet so taste, taste and taste again from here on in, adding as you go.

8 Batch cook the veg separately. Stir fried, steamed, fried, grilled, griddled, bbq, whatever you want. All is required at the end of this process is crunchy veg - very important not to overcook. The peppers and broccoli are ideally only lightly singed! Set aside.

9 Boil the noodles for a minute or two, then drain in cold water until they are no longer cooking. Empty back into the pan they were cooked in, add a little oil and stir through the cold noodles to stop them sticking together.

10 Add everything into the main soup pot – chicken, veg, noodles, the lot. Keep the pot on a medium heat to warm the dish through. Add a handful of coriander leaves and lime zest and serve into bowls.

Matt Carr
www.carrspasties.co.uk

Nicks Restaurant opened almost 20 years ago and we've been a proud part of the Bolton community ever since. As well as operating the restaurant 5 days a week, I also run cookery classes and cater for private events. I even find the time to do the odd radio show and cooking demo at Bolton Market every now and again!

Since beginning my chef career over 35 years ago, my passion has always been for creating fresh, simple food with emphasis on flavour and produce. A recipe doesn't have to be complicated and contain lots of ingredients in order to taste spectacular, you just need the right combination of flavours and good quality produce. Select ripe, seasonal fruit and vegetables and spend a little more money on your meat, fish and dairy products if possible. The end result will very much reflect the quality of ingredients you use.

I'm a real advocate of supporting local businesses and putting something back into the society in which we live and work. I like to encourage people to shop locally, try new things and be creative with seasonal produce.

Tuna Nicoise

SERVES 2

INGREDIENTS

2 tuna steaks (approx. 170g each)
6 boiled new potatoes
2 hard-boiled eggs
1 tbsp. capers
1 tbsp. black pitted olives
1 ripe tomatoes
1 pack watercress or rocket salad
50g green beans, cooked
Squeeze of lemon
Olive oil
Sea salt & black pepper

METHOD

1. Cut the potatoes, tomatoes and eggs into quarters and chop the beans into thirds. Mix together with all the salad ingredients and drizzle with a little olive oil and some freshly cracked black pepper.

2. Set a pan over a high heat. Drizzle the tuna in olive oil and sea salt and once the pan is really hot, cook for 3-4 minutes on each side. This should result in slightly pink tuna; cook for a few more minutes on each side if you prefer it more well-done.

3. Divide the salad mixture between 2 plates and arrange the tuna on top. Finish with a squeeze of lemon and serve.

Nicholas Cullen
https://www.facebook.com/nicksrestaurant
https://www.instagram.com/nicks_restaurant/

Northern Monkey brisket

SERVES 6

INGREDIENTS

1.8kg beef brisket joint,
   trimmed of fat
Salt to taste
2 large onion, sliced
330ml under dog from
   Northern monkey
2 tbsp dark brown soft
   sugar
1 beef stock cube, crumbled
2 tbsp freshly ground
   black pepper
2 tsp minced garlic
2 tbsp rich soy sauce
2 tbsp Lancashire sauce
1 bay leaf
¼ tsp dried thyme
2 tbsp cornflour mixed
   with 2 tbsp water
   (at the end of cooking)

METHOD

1 Preheat the oven to 180°C / Gas 4.

2 Season the beef brisket with salt, and place in a baking
   dish. Cover the entire joint with onion slices.

3 In a medium bowl, mix the beer, dark brown soft sugar,
   beef stock cube, pepper, garlic, soy sauce, bay leaf and
   thyme. Pour over the brisket. Cover with aluminum foil.

4 Bake for 4 hours in the preheated oven. The brisket
   should be fork-tender.

5 Mix together the cornflour and water; stir into the juices
   in the baking dish to thicken. Remove the bay leaf. Slice
   or rip apart the brisket with a couple of forks and serve
   on Lancashire oven bottoms with crumbled Lancashire
   cheese.

A little extra – Under dog bbq sauce

INGREDIENTS

16 tablespoons dark
   brown soft sugar
4 tablespoons mustard
   mild mustard
2 chillis chopped without
   seeds (leave the seeds in
   if you like it hot)
2 tsp Lancashire sauce
1 tsp rich soy sauce
2 peeled & finely chopped
   onion
½ teaspoon black pepper
220 ml under dog

METHOD

1 Mix all ingredients together in a saucepan and bring to
   the boil

2 Cook for 5 minutes, uncovered. If it's too runny mix
   1tbsp cornflour with 1 tbsp under dog, add and keep
   stirring for 2 minutes to cook out and thicken. Cool.
   Store in fridge till needed.

Mike Harrison
www.cheftogo.co.uk
www.northernmonkeybrew.co.uk

Cheese & Onion Pie

INGREDIENTS

Cheese pie filling

70g Unsalted Butter
125g Diced Onions
70g Plain Flour
280ml Whole Milk
280ml Double Cream
*625g VCP Mature
  Cheddar Cheese*
*2.5g Colman's English
  Mustard*
Egg Yolk

Shortcrust pastry

150g Unsalted Butter
150g Bako Shortening
600g Plain Flour
12g Table Salt
150ml Water

METHOD

Pastry

1   Place all the dry ingredients into the large mixing bowl and combine to a bread crumb.

2   Add the water to the dry combined mixed and bring together. Roll into a sausage and wrap with grease proof and chill for about 1 hour.

Filling

1   Cube the cheese ready for use.

2   Melt the butter in the large pan.

3   Add the onions and cook without colouring them.

4   Add the flour to make a roux.

5   Warm the milk and cream and add slowly.

6   Melt the cubed cheese in the microwave until soft.

7   Empty the cubed cheese and stir, continue to cook for a further 5 mins until all the cheese has melted.

8   Mix in the mustard and egg.

9   Allow to cool in a big tub.

Pie tin

1   Use butter to grease the pie tin/s and flour.

2   Roll the pastry flat and place on the tin/s.

3   Place the cheese filling inside the pie.

4   Egg wash a lid and cover the base and filling.

5   Egg wash the outside.

6   Cook for around 25min at 200°C.

Scott Bannon
www.boarsheadhoghton.com

Beef Pot Roast

INGREDIENTS

750g beef joint I use silverside

Olive oil

2 sticks celery, chopped into large chunks

4 carrots, peeled, chopped into large chunks

5 Shallots, peeled and sliced

6 cloves of garlic, peeled and crushed

300ml red wine

250ml beef stock

4 bay leaves

1 tbsp dried oregano

2 Sprogs Thyme

1 tbsp cornflour

50g Butter

METHOD

1 Either prepare your slow cooker or Preheat your oven to 180°C.

2 Rub olive oil all over the beef and then season the joint well with Maldon sea salt & black pepper.

3 Heat 1 tbsp of oil in a frying pan then add the joint and brown it on all sides. Put it in a casserole dish or slow cooker, make sure it's large enough to fit the joint and all the vegetables.

4 In the same pan add your butter, some olive oil and once hot add your shallots, gently dust over your cornflour and cook out for 5-6 minutes before adding to your casserole dish.

5 Add another tbsp of oil to the frying pan then brown all the chopped vegetables.

6 Arrange them around the joint in the casserole pot/slow cooker.

7 Add the crushed garlic cloves, red wine, Beef Stock, bay leaves and dried oregano to the casserole and bring to the boil.

8 Cover the casserole with a lid and cook in the preheated oven for 2 hours, turning the meat over halfway. Serve with Roast or Mashed Potatoes.

Simon Wood 2015 MasterChef Champion
Chef Patron at WOOD Restaurants
www.woodrestaurantgroup.com

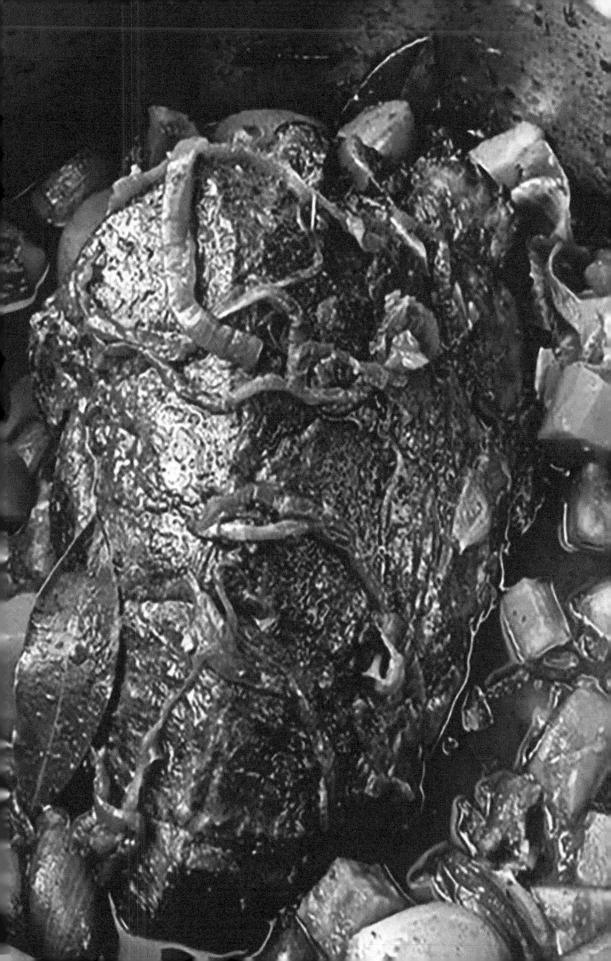

Mughlai Kadhai Paneer

SERVES 4 PEOPLE

INGREDIENTS

450 gms paneer diced bite
size chunks

3 tbsp vegetable oil

120g white onion finely
chopped

4 cloves garlic finely
chopped

400g tomato roughly
chopped

3 tbsp tomato puree

1 tsp kashmiri chilli
powder or mild paprika

¼ tsp turmeric powder

3 tbsp Greek yoghurt

200 mls water

2" medium size peppers
diced squares

80g red onion diced
squares

Salt to taste

1 tbsp methi/dried crushed
fenugreek seeds

1" ginger juliennes

Coriander to garnish

For the Kadhai Masala

2 dried mild kashmiri
chillies

2 tbsp coriander seeds

2 tsp cumin seeds

1 tsp black pepper

8 green cardamom
seeds only

Kishan Shah, Sai spice
www.saispice.co.uk

METHOD

1   In a dry frying pan add the kadhai masala spices and
heat over a low flame. Give the pan a shake every few
seconds. Roast for a 2-3 minutes. Cool and grind to a
coarse powder and set aside.

2   Add the tomatoes and tomato puree to a blender and
blitz to a smooth paste.

3   In a heavy bottom non stick sauce pan or kadhai heat
the oil over a medium flame. Add 1 tablespoon of the
ground kadhai masala and fry for a few seconds. Add
the onions and fry for 12 minutes. Make sure to stir well
and scrap the bottom of the pan

4   Add the garlic and continue to fry for a minute. Add
the tomato paste and fry over a medium heat for 12-14
minutes. You want the sauce to reduce slightly and
thicken. Add the kashmiri chilli powder and turmeric
powder stir well for a minute.

5   Now turn the heat to a low setting and add the yoghurt a
little at a time. Stir well continuously for 4 minutes.

6   Turn the heat back to a medium and add the peppers
and red onion and fry for 6-7 minutes. Add another
tablespoon of the kadhai masala and crushed kasoori
methi. Season to taste.

7   Add the paneer and stir well coating the paneer in the
gravy. Cook for 3 minutes as the paneer begins to soften.
Turn the heat off and garnish with ginger and coriander.
Serve with naan and salad.

Balti burger and roast potato wedges

SERVES 4

INGREDIENTS

For the burgers

1 tablespoon vegetable oil

2 spring onions, finely
   chopped

1 clove garlic, crushed

1 red chilli, seeds removed
   if you prefer

450g lean lamb mince
   (or beef if you prefer)

1 tablespoon fresh mint,
   roughly chopped

2 tablespoons Pataks
   Balti paste

1 egg

4 burger buns or pitta
   bread toasted

Salad for the burgers

For the Roast
Potato Wedges

1 kg new potatoes, I love
   Charlotte potatoes,
   cut into wedges

Good drizzle of olive oil

1 teaspoon cumin seeds

1 teaspoon smoked paprika

4 cloves of garlic,
   left in their skins

Good pinch of sea salt and
   cracked black pepper

For the dip

4 tablespoons crème fraiche

2 tablespoons Brinjal
   Pickle (I suggest Pataks)

1 tablespoon chives, chopped

METHOD

1   Put the potato wedges on for roasting. Mix all the
    ingredients together in a roasting tray and roast in a
    preheated oven (180°C) for 45 minutes or until cooked
    through and golden brown.

2   In the meantime make the Balti burgers. Gently heat the
    oil in a pan and add the spring onions, garlic and red
    chilli. After a minute or so remove from the heat.

3   In a large bowl mix together the lamb mince, fresh mint,
    Balti Paste and spring onion mix. Divide into 4 large
    patties. If you have time place on a tray, cover with cling
    film and chill for an hour to set the shape.

4   Heat a griddle pan and cook, turning them over, for
    around 10 minutes, or until fully cooked through.

5   Mix the crème fraiche with Brinjal Pickle and chives.

6   Place some iceberg lettuce in a bun topped with a burger
    and serve with Roast Potato Wedges and spicy dip.

Anjali Pathak
www.anjalipathak.com

Fish tacos

INGREDIENTS

125ml sour cream

125ml mayonnaise

½ bunch chopped fresh coriander

heaped tbsp taco seasoning mix (recipe below)

500g cod loin or ask what's on offer from your fishmonger, cut into 1-inch pieces

2 tbsp vegetable oil

2 tbsp lemon juice

12 taco shells, warmed

Homemade taco seasoning – blend and top the fish tacos

1 tbsp Chilli Powder

¼ tsp Garlic Powder

¼ tsp Onion Powder

¼ tsp Dried Oregano

½ tsp Paprika

½ tsp Ground Cumin

1 tsp Sea Salt

1 tsp Black Pepper (optional)

TOPPINGS

Shredded cos lettuce

Chopped tomato

Sliced red onion

Lime juice

Taco sauce

METHOD

1 Combine sour cream, mayonnaise, coriander and 2 tbsp seasoning mix in small bowl.

2 Combine fish, vegetable oil, lemon juice and remaining seasoning mix in medium bowl; pour into large frying pan.

3 Cook, stirring gently but constantly, over medium-high heat for 4 to 5 minutes or until cod flakes easily when tested with a fork.

4 Fill taco shells with fish mixture, and top with choice of toppings and sour cream.

Baking Nannas Coffee &
Walnut Cake with Cheesecake Filling

INGREDIENTS

Cake

225g Soft Brown Sugar
225g Stork/Butter
4 Eggs
225g Self Raising Flour
50g Chopped Walnuts
3 tablespoons of Camp
  Coffee

Cheesecake Filling
& Topping

180g Philadelphia Cream
  Cheese
300mls Double Cream
120g Icing Sugar
1 tablespoon of Camp
  Coffee
Walnuts (to decorate)

METHOD

1 Preheat your oven to 160°C fan. Make the cake first by creaming the Stork/Butter with the brown sugar then whisk in the eggs one at a time. 2.Add the camp coffee, walnuts & self-raising flour and proceed to fold slowly until they are all combined.

2 Divide the mixture between two 8" lined and greased loose bottomed cake tins and bake for 35/40 minutes. Once this is done, leave them to go cold on a wire cooling rack.

3 Once you have done this, make your cheesecake by whisking the cream cheese, camp coffee & icing sugar together, then add the double cream and whisk until you have a very firm mousse, ideally using an electric hand whisk.

4 Fill and top your cake with it and decorate with the extra walnuts. 6.Place the cake in the fridge for at least 3 hours to give the cheesecake time to firm up, even better overnight.

@CAMPCOFFEEUK

Biscoff Tiramisu

◆

APPROX 4 SERVINGS

INGREDIENTS

250ml double cream
250g mascarpone
125g caster sugar
Coffee extract 2tsp
Vanilla extract 1tsp
Biscoff biscuits 1 pack
½ pint milk to quick soak biscuits in.
Jar biscoff spread
Cocoa powder to dust

METHOD

1. Start by whipping the cream until almost fully whipped.
2. Add the mascarpone/ vanilla/ coffee extract.
3. Mix in thoroughly then gradually add caster sugar to desired sweetness.
4. Melt 2tbsp biscoff spread in microwave until it becomes pouring consistency.
5. Get your preferred dish ready and start by dipping the biscuits in the milk and creating your first layer of biscuit.
6. Then a smooth even layer of the cream mix.
7. Little drizzle of the biscoff spread.
8. Repeat at least 3 to 4 times till your happy with the quantity.
9. Your top layer should finish with a nice smooth cream mix. Then dust with cocoa powder until covered.
10. Place in fridge to set for approximately 2 to 3 hours.

Gareth Mason
www.retreatrestaurants.co.uk
Facebook Gareth Mason, Next level events.

The best chocolate fudge cake ever!

INGREDIENTS

175g self raising flour
3tbsp cocoa powder
2 tbsp golden syrup
175g caster sugar
2 eggs, beaten
1 tsp bicarbonate soda
1 tsp baking powder
6 tbsp veg oil
6 tbsp hot water

METHOD

1 Pre heat your oven to 170°C.

2 Mix the flour, cocoa powder, caster sugar, bicarb and baking powder together. Add the beaten eggs and golden syrup and mix. Put the oil and hot water in a jug and then add to the mix and whisk with an electric mixer for no more than 1 minute.

3 Divide between two 8" round tins and bake in the centre of your pre heated oven for 25-30 minutes. Then allow to cool.

INGREDIENTS

Chocolate fudge topping
10 tbsp butter softened
275g cocoa powder
775g icing sugar
160ml warm milk
2 tsp vanilla extract

METHOD

1 Mix the softened butter with the cocoa powder and icing sugar, add the warm milk a little at a time until a thick spreadable consistency is achieved, add the vanilla extract.

2 Spread generously between the two sponges, stack and spread the topping over the top and sides of the cake using a palette knife.

3 Place in the fridge for at least 30 minutes to firm up, one slice and it will be gone!

Chocolate fudge cake by Natasha Lees
Octagon kitchen & bar
www.octagonbolton.co.uk

Apple Tart Tatin

(Other fruit can be used).

INGREDIENTS

100g butter
200g caster sugar
Water
6 Granny Smith apples
6 star anise
3 vanilla pods, halved
12 cardamom pods
3 cinnamon sticks
300g puff pastry –
  Ready Rolled

METHOD

1 Preheat the oven to 180°C.

2 Line deep tart tins with greaseproof paper.

3 Using a large oven proof frying pan (approx. 28cm) gently melt the butter on a medium heat with the star anise vanilla pod and cardamom pods and then add the sugar. Gently colour everything until it is pale yellow in colour.

4 Bring to a simmer and boil for approximately 5 minutes, without stirring, or until you have a rich golden brown caramel.

5 Pour the caramel into the bases of the tart tins.

6 Put one star anise, half vanilla pod, half cinnamon stick and a couple of cardamom pods in the caramel.

7 Peel the apples and place in the centre of the tin.

8 Roll out the pastry and cut into discs large enough to totally cover the apple.

9 Cover the apple, tucking the edges of the pastry down the sides, making sure it touches the caramel

10 Place the tarts to the oven and bake for 20/30 minutes, until the pastry is crisp and golden and the apples are soft when a knife is inserted into them.

11 Leave to cool slightly, then invert onto serving plates and serve with a scoop of vanilla or caramel ice cream.

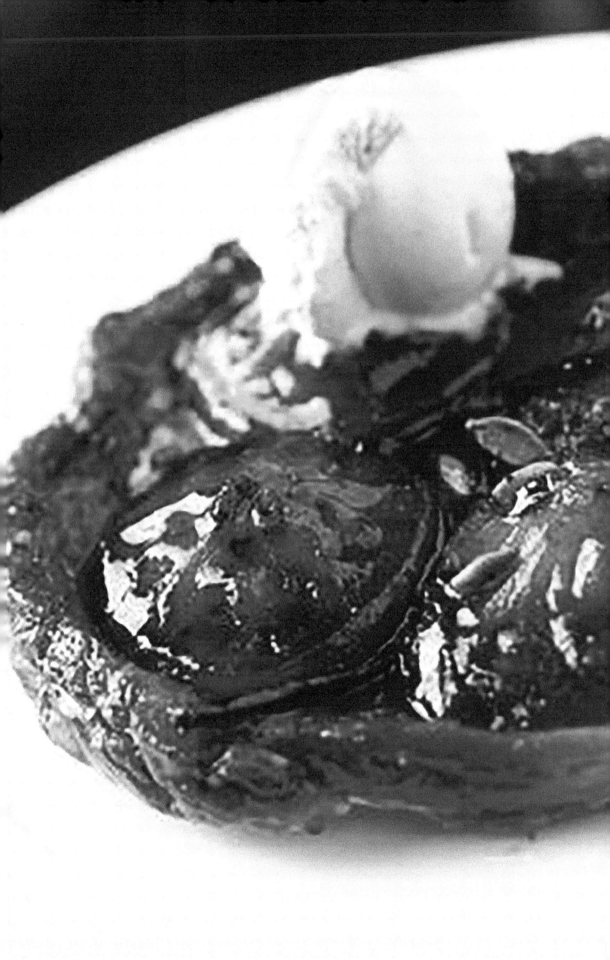

Vimto trifle

*300ml hot vimto as
     strong as you like*
6 leaves gelatine
200g sponge fingers
100g raspberries
100g blackcurrants
100g blackberries
700ml cream
4 egg yolks
1 vanilla pod
30g caster sugar
1 tsp cornflour
50g flaked almonds

METHOD

1. Soak the gelatine in cold water until soft, drain and add to the hot vimto.

2. Place the sponge fingers in your bowl top with the fruit, pour on the vimto and leave to cool then place in the fridge to set.

3. Make the custard by heating 300ml of the cream and vanilla to just below a simmer.

4. Whisk together the sugar, cornflour and egg yolks in a bowl, pour on the warm cream and whisk again to mix.

5. Return the cream mix to the pan and cook out on a low heat to thicken.

6. Allow to cool and then pour over the set jelly.

7. Whip the remaining cream to soft peak and use to top the trifle then sprinkle with almonds.

Robert Owen Brown
www.thehinchliffe.co.uk

Meet the Mayor's charities

Octagon Theatre – regional and local theatre at the heart of Bolton's town centre. Established 50 years ago and run completely as a charity.

Urban Outreach – meeting the needs of all through high quality services of support preventing homelessness and co-ordinating the Food Hub, a foodbank which is open to anyone in need in the town.

BACKUP North West – aims to prevent homelessness among 16-25 year olds by providing supported furnished housing and support to encourage independent living.

Fortalice – A Bolton refuge that offers emotional and practical support for women fleeing domestic abuse.

HALLIWELL BEFRIENDING SERVICE

Halliwell Befriending Service – a service ran by volunteers to offer support to the elderly in their homes and prevent isolation.

Bolton's business referral networking group

rich@straightlinecommunications.co.uk

emily.mort@icinsurance.co.uk

gill@wrenaccounting.co.uk

joe@ownyourspace.co.uk

ian@boltonkitchens.co.uk

info@rosealexanderproperty.com

info@chameleonbdsltd.co.uk

janwebb@cornerstoneoh.co.uk

marcus@totaldigitalsolutionsgroup.com

airborneservices22@gmail.com

Thank you to the 10 local businesses, members of BNI,
for sponsoring the Mayor's Charity 2020/21.

We own, manage and maintain more than 18,000 homes across the borough.

We invest to improve the quality of our properties and are building new homes to give as many people as we can the opportunity to live in a quality, affordable home.

Our work goes far beyond bricks and mortar. We tackle poverty with debt and money advice. We provide food and clothes initiatives and help people keep warm for less. We support tenants and residents into training and employment, and deal with antisocial behaviour and domestic abuse.

We help customers to remain independent in their own homes with a community alarm service and adaptations. And we work with volunteer groups to build sustainable communities.

We're a charitable community benefit society that works to make people's lives better by providing quality housing, giving people opportunities to prosper and helping customers to maximise their income. To achieve this we work in partnership with a variety of local charities, social enterprises and other agencies.

Phone: **01204 328000**
Facebook: **@fbboltonathome**
Twitter: **@boltonathome**
Website: **www.boltonathome.org.uk**

Bolton at Home

FEATURING
RANDING

FEATURING
STRATEGY

FEATURING
FILM

FEATURING
DIGITAL

FEATURING
CAMPAIGN

DESIGNED TO
REACH AUDIENCES

Maxmedia.

DESIGN
WITH
PURPOSE

IMPROVE
LIVES

INSPIRE
POSITIVE
CHANGE

STORY BY:
YOU

DIRECTED BY:
US

PRODUCED BY:
COLLABORATION

01200 438 160   WWW.MAX-MEDIAGROUP.CO.UK

Acknowledgements

A special thank you to all the gourmet chefs and
establishments who have contributed such fantastic recipes.

Mike Harrison – Chef to Go

Sushma Solanki – Sushma Snacks

Michael Caines MBE – Lympstone Manor

Tom Bridge – Pie Society

Colin Unsworth – Forest Horizons

Matt Carr – Carr's Pasties

Nicholas Cullen – Nick's Restaurant

Scott Bannon – Boar's Head Hoghton

Simon Wood – Wood Restaurants

Kishan Shah – Sai Spice

Anjali Pathak

Jackie Heaton

Gareth Mason – Retreat Restaurants

Natasha Lees – Octagon Kitchen Bar

Jean Christophe Novelli

Robert Owen Brown – The Hinchcliffe

Northern Monkey

The Cherry Tree, Blackrod

Camp Coffee UK

Thank you to the generous sponsors for their support of this book.

BNI – Rich Williams, President of Bolton Chapter

Bolton@Home

Maxmedia

A Sincere Thanks to All

Much gratitude to our Mayor's team making
it possible for this publication to be made,
Especially David, Mary and Ade.

Thank you Mike Harrison, and many a gourmet cook,
Contributing recipes in our charitable book.

We are indebted to Emma Lori's graphic and editorial layout,
And all those enabling this to come about.

Lightning Source UK Ltd.
Milton Keynes UK
UKHW021124221220
375694UK00003B/31

9 781783 241804